5/15

P9-CEE-594

~LYNNFIELD PUBLIC LIBRARY~
LYNNFIELD, MA 01940

Planet
Uranus

CHRISTINE TAYLOR-BUTLER

Children's Press®
An Imprint of Scholastic Inc.
New York Toronto London Auckland Sydney
Mexico City New Delhi Hong Kong
Danbury, Connecticut

-LYNNFIELD PUBLIC LIBRARY-
LYNNFIELD, MA 01940

Content Consultant
Bryan C. Dunne
Assistant Chair, Assistant Professor, Department of Astronomy
University of Illinois at Urbana–Champaign
Urbana, Illinois

Library of Congress Cataloging-in-Publication Data
Taylor-Butler, Christine.
 Planet Uranus / by Christine Taylor-Butler.
  pages cm. — (A true book)
 Audience: Ages 9–12.
 Audience: Grades 4–6.
 ISBN 978-0-531-21158-8 (lib. bdg.) — ISBN 978-0-531-25364-9 (pbk.)
 1. Uranus (Planet)—Juvenile literature. I. Title. II. Series: True book.
 QB681.T39 2014
 523.47—dc23   2013027622

No part of this publication may be reproduced in whole or in part, or stored in a retrieval system, or transmitted in any form or by any means, electronic, mechanical, photocopying, recording, or otherwise, without written permission of the publisher. For information regarding permission, write to Scholastic Inc., Attention: Permissions Department, 557 Broadway, New York, NY 10012.

© 2014 Scholastic Inc.

All rights reserved. Published in 2014 by Children's Press, an imprint of Scholastic Inc.
Printed in China 62
SCHOLASTIC, CHILDREN'S PRESS, A TRUE BOOK™, and associated logos are trademarks and/or registered trademarks of Scholastic Inc.

1 2 3 4 5 6 7 8 9 10 R 23 22 21 20 19 18 17 16 15 14

Front cover: The *Voyager 2* spacecraft approaching Uranus

Back cover: Uranus, as seen from its moon Miranda

Find the Truth!

Everything you are about to read is true *except* for one of the sentences on this page.

Which one is **TRUE**?

T or F   Uranus's core is frozen.

T or F   *Voyager 2* is the only spacecraft to ever visit Uranus.

Find the answers in this book.

Contents

THE **BIG** TRUTH!

**Astronomer Gerard Kuiper discovered
Uranus's moon Miranda.**

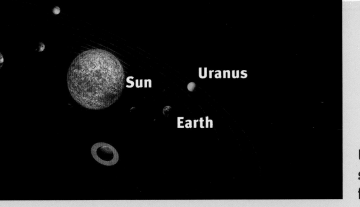

Sun

Uranus

Earth

Uranus is the seventh planet from the sun.

The *Voyager 2* spacecraft was launched before its twin, *Voyager 1*.

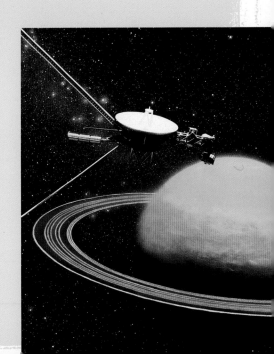

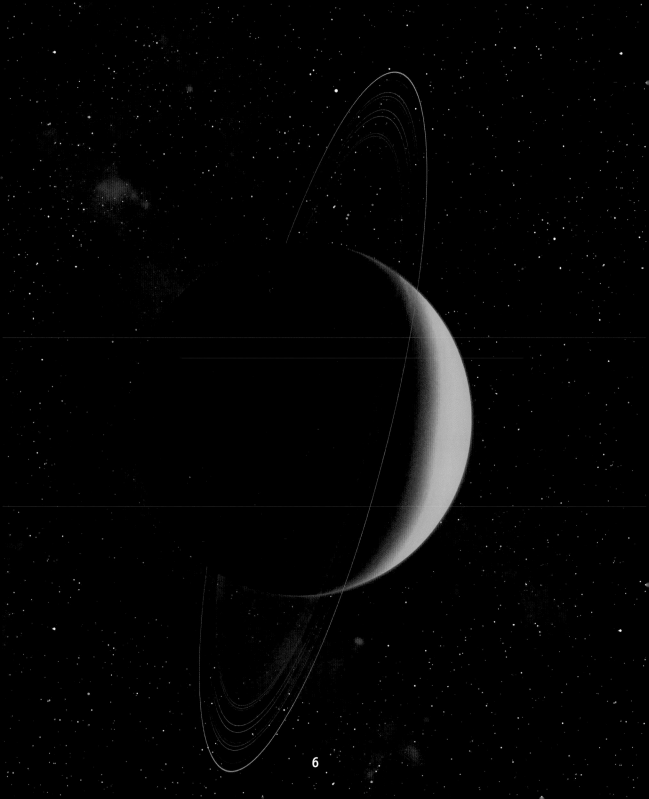

CHAPTER 1

The Sideways Planet

At first glance, Uranus may not look very interesting. In fact, **astronomers** were disappointed at their first close-up view of the **planet** in 1986. Uranus appeared to be only a blue-green ball with a smooth surface. But as scientists learned more, they realized that nothing about the planet was ordinary. Its magnetic field and rotation were much different than Earth's. Uranus's unusual blue-green color is sunlight reflected from methane gas in the planet's **atmosphere**.

Uranus is named for the Greek sky god and first ruler of the mythological Titans.

Far and Dark

Uranus **orbits** the sun, just like the other seven planets in our solar system. It is the seventh from the sun. Uranus is too far away to see easily without a telescope. However, sometimes it is just bright enough to see with the naked eye. Uranus may be spotted in the early morning during the summer. It also appears at night in the fall and in the early evening during winter months.

Uranus can just barely be seen in the sky above Mars in this photo.

Uranus

Mars

8

Uranus is almost four times bigger around than Earth.

Uranus may be hard to see, but that does not mean it is small. Uranus is the third-largest planet in the solar system. It has the fourth-largest **mass**. If you measured around the planet at its **equator**, it would measure 99,018 miles (159,354 kilometers) around. By comparison, Earth is only 24,873 miles (40,029 km) around.

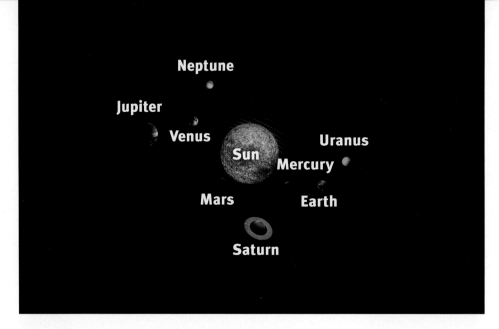

Our solar system includes eight planets.

Uranus is so far away from the sun that it takes 84 Earth years for it to complete one orbit. Because Uranus's orbit is **elliptical**, its distance from the sun changes. At its closest, it is 1.7 billion miles (2.7 billion km) away. At its farthest, it is 1.9 billion miles (3.1 billion km) away. The distance from Uranus to Earth also changes. When on the same side of the sun, the planets are 1.6 billion miles (2.6 billion km) away from each other. When they are on opposite sides, they are 2 billion miles (3.2 billion km) apart.

Unusual Rotation

Uranus is tipped 98 degrees to the side. This means its north and south poles are almost perpendicular to all other planets in our solar system. For half of Uranus's orbit, one **hemisphere** points toward the sun. For the other half of the orbit, the other hemisphere points toward the sun. Scientists believe a large body in space, such as a giant asteroid, may have hit Uranus. The impact could have knocked the planet on its side.

Most planets spin standing up like a top, as shown by the orange planet. Uranus, the blue planet, rotates on its side.

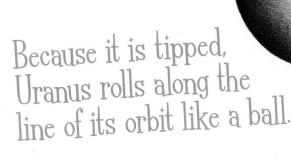

Because it is tipped, Uranus rolls along the line of its orbit like a ball.

Each of Uranus's hemispheres receives 42 Earth years of sunlight. This is followed by 42 Earth years of darkness. Like Earth, Uranus has four seasons. But on Uranus, a season lasts 21 Earth years. Scientists have observed that as seasons change, clouds in areas moving from winter to spring become bigger and brighter. Similarly, clouds lose some of their strength in regions changing to fall and winter.

The next time the north pole of Uranus will point toward the sun is in 2028.

Each of Uranus's hemispheres goes through a long period without sunlight every year.

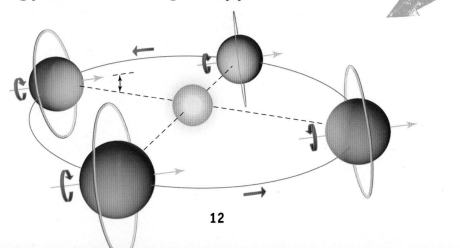

12

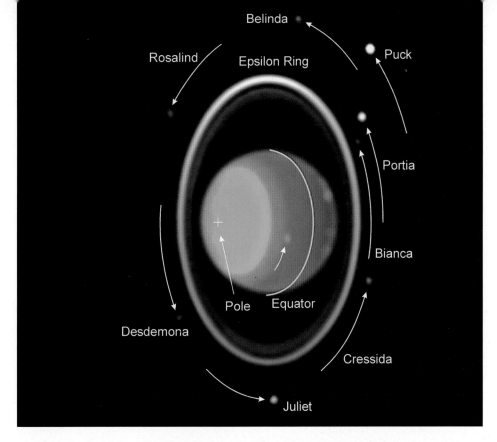

Belinda

Rosalind

Epsilon Ring

Puck

Portia

Bianca

Pole   Equator

Desdemona

Cressida

Juliet

Uranus's moons orbit in the same direction Uranus rotates.

Uranus is one of two planets in our solar system that spins clockwise. The other planet is Venus. Earth and the remaining planets rotate counterclockwise. Uranus also spins quite fast. One day on Uranus lasts only about 17 hours. Clouds in its atmosphere flow even faster in some areas. They complete one rotation in an average of 14 hours.

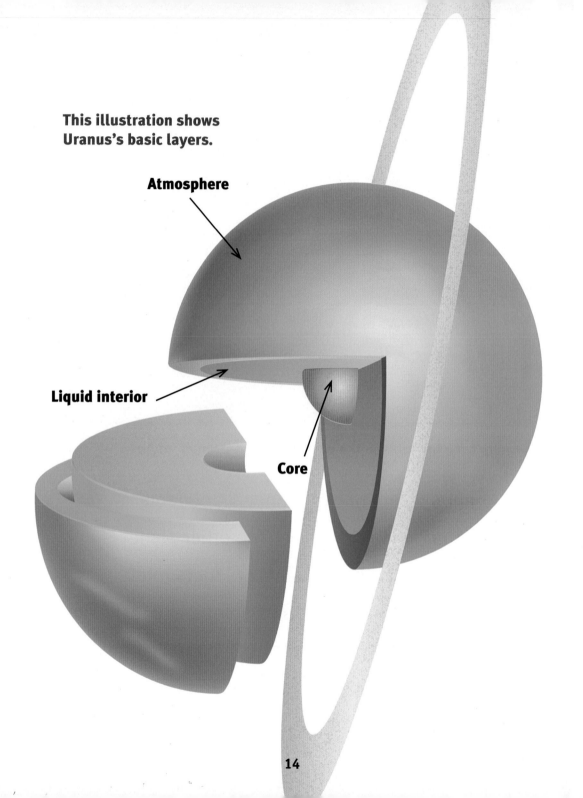

This illustration shows Uranus's basic layers.

Atmosphere

Liquid interior

Core

CHAPTER 2

Ices and Gases

Uranus is sometimes called a gas giant and an ice giant. Gas and ice giants do not have a solid surface surrounding their rocky **core**. Around its core, Uranus is liquid. This liquid is under enormous pressure. It is composed of water, ammonia, and methane. Above the liquid layer, hydrogen, helium, and methane gases form the planet's thick atmosphere.

A large storm spotted on Uranus in 2006 was two-thirds the size of the United States.

Cool Blue Planet

Uranus is far from the sun, so it is very cold. The temperature at the cloudtops averages −357 degrees Fahrenheit (−216 degrees Celsius). At its core, the temperature is higher. Some scientists estimate that it is around 8,500°F (4,700°C). This is hot, but it is much cooler than Jupiter's core temperature of 43,000°F (24,000°C). Unlike other planets, Uranus does not radiate much heat from its interior out into space.

As one of Uranus's hemispheres turns away from the sun the temperature there drops.

16

Like all gas giants in our solar system, Uranus's atmosphere is mostly hydrogen and helium.

Uranus's atmosphere is 82.5 percent hydrogen, 15.2 percent helium, and 2.3 percent methane. That small amount of methane is what gives the planet its smooth blue-green appearance. The temperature is warmer in the upper atmosphere. This is because the top layer absorbs a tiny amount of heat from the sun. But it is still cold. Uranus's outermost layer is about −243°F (−153°C).

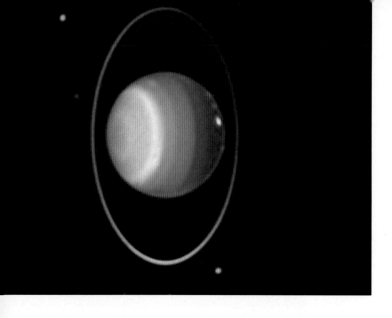

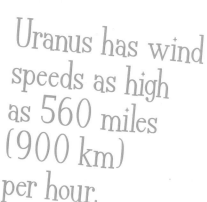

Uranus has wind speeds as high as 560 miles (900 km) per hour.

Cloudy Weather

Is there weather on Uranus? Absolutely! However, scientists did not realize the severity of the weather at first. The *Voyager 2* spacecraft flew by the planet in 1986. The spacecraft detected clouds in the lower atmosphere. The Hubble Space Telescope later confirmed it in the 1990s. Storms are most active during the planet's equinox. An equinox happens when the sun shines directly on a planet's equator. Then the sun's light reaches both hemispheres equally.

Lightweight

Uranus has 15 times the mass of Earth. However, it is much less **dense** than Earth is. As a result, you would weigh a little less on Uranus than you do on Earth. Scientists have measured Uranus's gravity by studying how it affects the planet's moons. Scientists also measured how the gravity affected *Voyager 2* as it flew by Uranus.

The moon Ariel casts a shadow as it orbits Uranus. Scientists can calculate Uranus's gravity by studying the orbits of its moons.

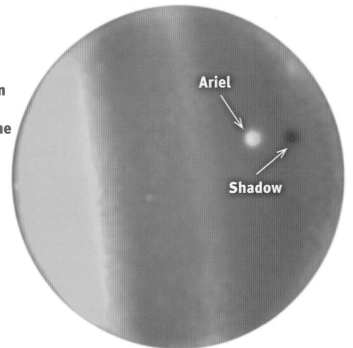

Ariel

Shadow

Unusual Magnetism

Like most planets, Uranus has a magnetic field. Earth's magnetic field is more or less in line with its **axis**. However, Uranus's magnetic field is tilted about 59 degrees away from its axis. The magnetic field is also not lined up with the center of the planet. That means your compass would not point anywhere near the north and south poles. The only other planet with such an odd magnetic field is Neptune.

Unlike most planets, Uranus's magnetic field is off-center and nowhere near its axis.

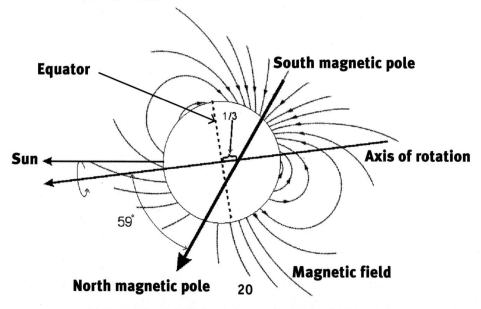

Equator

South magnetic pole

1/3

Sun

Axis of rotation

59°

Magnetic field

North magnetic pole

Honeycomb Mirrors

Uranus is billions of miles away from Earth. How can we see so far away? By looking through a powerful telescope. One example is the W. M. Keck Observatory on Mauna Kea in Hawaii. It houses two telescopes. Each has a 400-inch (10-meter) mirror. A single mirror that size is too expensive to build. So each large mirror is made of 36 smaller, honeycomb-shaped mirrors. The telescopes can see objects that are 10 billion light-years away. This is about 588 trillion miles (946 trillion km).

Mirrors

Mysterious Miranda

The tiny moon Miranda was discovered orbiting Uranus in 1948. It is the closest known moon to Uranus and is only 293 miles (472 km) across. But its origin remains a mystery.

A large impact may have shattered Miranda.

Miranda looks like it was assembled with mismatched parts. The surface is covered in cracks. The cracks are 12 times deeper than Earth's Grand Canyon. Was the moon shattered by a massive impact and did the pieces come back together, as shown in the diagram on page 22? Did meteoroid strikes shape its surface? Scientists do not know for sure.

Miranda is named for the only female character in William Shakespeare's play The Tempest.

Astronomer Gerard Kuiper found Miranda while studying photographs at McDonald Observatory in Texas.

Titania

Umbriel

Portia → Miranda

Puck

Ariel

Oberon

CHAPTER 3

Natural Satellites

Uranus does not have a solid surface. But it does have a lot of satellites that have solid surfaces. Satellites are objects such as moons that orbit another, larger object. Six years after Uranus was first discovered, astronomers found two moons. They named the moons Titania and Oberon. After that, it was a long time before any more moons were seen. Now the Hubble telescope gives astronomers a closer look at Uranus's satellites.

Uranus's moons are named after characters created by writers William Shakespeare and Alexander Pope.

Titania

Titania is Uranus's largest moon. Its radius is 490.1 miles (788.7 km). *Voyager 2* took a close look at the moon's surface of rock and ice. The spacecraft discovered cracks and valleys that are as long as 1,000 miles (1,600 km). The moon also has fewer craters than other moons of its size. This may mean that Titania has earthquakes or other geologic activity. Over time, this activity would smooth out the moon's surface and cover craters.

Like all known moons orbiting Uranus, Titania is a gray color.

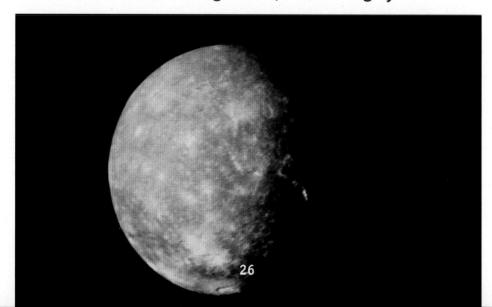

26

Titania and Oberon are named for the queen and king of the fairies in Shakespeare's *A Midsummer Night's Dream.*

Although it was first seen through a telescope in 1787, scientists did not know much about the moon Oberon until *Voyager 2* flew by it.

Oberon

Uranus's second-largest moon is named Oberon. Its radius is 473 miles (761 km). Like Titania, its surface is made up of ice and rock. It is covered with craters, many more than Titania. *Voyager 2* spotted a mountain almost 4 miles (6.4 km) high when it passed the moon in 1986. There may be other mountains that scientists have not seen.

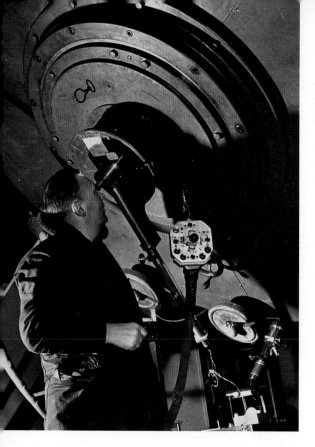

Gerard Kuiper peers through a telescope at McDonald Observatory in West Texas.

More Moons

In the 1850s, William Lassell discovered the moons Ariel and Umbriel. Ariel is Uranus's brightest moon. Umbriel is dark. Then, in 1948, Gerard Kuiper discovered Miranda. Almost 40 years passed before *Voyager 2* discovered 10 more moons in 1986. Those moons were very small, ranging from 16 to 96 miles (26 to 154 km) wide. They were named Juliet, Puck, Cordelia, Ophelia, Bianca, Desdemona, Portia, Rosalind, Cressida, and Belinda.

Since its launch into space, Hubble has brought the total of known moons to 27. The most recent of these moons were found in 2005. That year, photos taken by Hubble revealed two new moons. Tiny Cupid orbits among a cluster of moons around Uranus's middle rings. Mab orbits farther out, along Uranus's outermost ring. Scientists believe Mab is the source of the dust in the ring. In 2006, Hubble photos showed a sight never seen before: Ariel's shadow passing across Uranus.

This illustration shows the orbits of Uranus's known moons with dotted lines. Ring locations are highlighted in blue, red, and solid white lines.

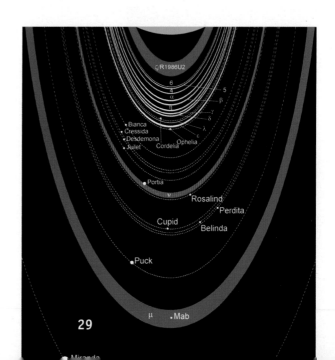

Rings Around the Planet

Uranus's rings were not discovered until 1977. Two scientific teams noticed that light from a star began to flicker just before and just after Uranus passed in front of it. A closer look revealed rings orbiting the planet. One team counted five rings. They named them Alpha, Beta, Gamma, Delta, and Epsilon. The other team counted six rings and numbered them 1 through 6 instead.

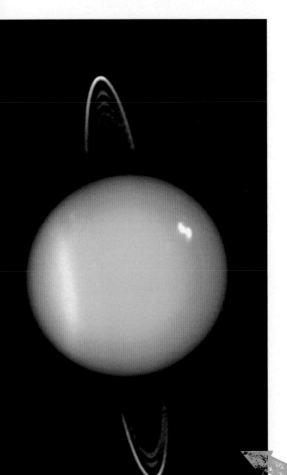

Unlike rings orbiting other planets, Uranus's rings wobble.

Color was added to Uranus's rings in this image to make them easier to see. The color also highlights wide bands of fine dust particles filling the space between the rings.

Combining their findings, the scientists identified nine unique rings. In 1986, the *Voyager 2* spacecraft discovered two more rings. This brought the total to 11. Then, in 2005, images from Hubble revealed two additional rings. As of 2013, Uranus has 13 known rings. The planet's inner 11 rings are narrow and dark. They are impossible to see without high-powered telescopes. The outer two rings are comparatively brighter. However, they are still hard to see.

Uranus's rings are a mix of large chunks of matter and tiny particles of dust.

The rings orbiting Uranus are thinner than those orbiting other planets. Many of the rings are made up mostly of dust. This dust reflects only small amounts of light. Other rings contain boulders as large as trucks. Scientists believe the debris may have come from a small moon. The moon was destroyed in a collision with another object, and its pieces formed rings.

Astronomers noticed something new when they compared images from *Voyager 2* and Hubble. *Voyager 2* had shown the horizontal plane of the rings facing Earth. But Uranus does not always face this way. As Uranus orbits the sun, the planet and its rings are seen from different angles. By 2007, only the edges of the rings were visible from Earth. We see these edges every 42 years.

This edge-on photo of Uranus's rings was taken by astronomers at the Keck Observatory in Hawaii.

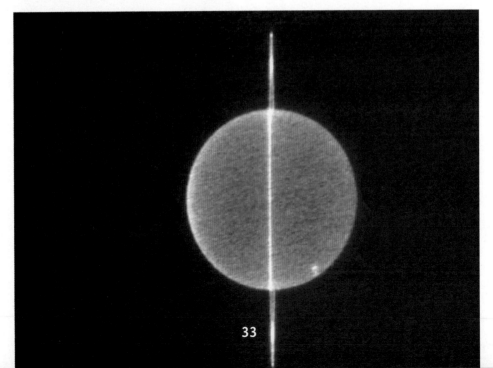

Astronomer William Herschel worked closely with his sister Caroline.

Astronomer William Herschel built his own telescopes to look at the stars.

34

CHAPTER 4

An Unusual Discovery

Ancient astronomers studied some planets in the sky. They could see five planets with the naked eye. The ancient Romans named those planets after their gods: Mercury, Venus, Mars, Jupiter, and Saturn. But Uranus was not among them. Until the late 1700s, no one knew it existed. That all changed when an astronomer with a hand-built telescope looked at the sky.

Something New

In 1781, astronomer William Herschel was studying the stars. He noticed one that did not behave like the others. At first, he thought it might be a **comet**. But the object did not behave like a comet. He named this object in honor of the king of England, George III. He called it Georgium Sidus, which means George's Star in Latin. Not long afterward, scientists determined the object was a planet. With this discovery, astronomers agreed to name the planet Uranus, after the Greek god of the sky.

Uranus (left) is pictured here with Vesta, the Roman goddess of the family hearth, or fireplace.

The British Nautical Almanac continued to call Uranus "Georgium Sidus" until 1850.

William Herschel is shown here holding a diagram of Uranus and the two moons he discovered.

Six years later, William Herschel discovered two moons orbiting Uranus. These moons did not seem to orbit the way our moon orbits Earth. These moons appeared to be circling the planet's north and south poles. Herschel concluded that Uranus was tipped on its side. After Herschel's death, his son, John, named the moons Titania and Oberon.

High-powered telescopes at the Keck Observatory in Hawaii create detailed images of Uranus.

Visiting Uranus

There is still much we do not know about Uranus. It is billions of miles away, which makes it difficult to study. But we are always developing new technology. Data from telescopes both on Earth and in space are helping scientists to understand this cold, mysterious planet. One spacecraft has managed to visit Uranus. But it took a little creativity to get it there.

 The Keck Observatory is built on top of a dormant volcano.

Voyage Into Space

In 1977, Jupiter, Saturn, Uranus, and Neptune lined up. A spacecraft could use each planet's gravity to change course and continue on to the next planet. Scientists designed two remote-controlled spacecraft named *Voyager 1* and *Voyager 2*. The spacecraft would visit Saturn and Jupiter. The *Voyagers* were designed to operate for only five years. But both spacecraft continued to function longer than planned. Seizing the opportunity, scientists programmed *Voyager 2* to visit Uranus, too.

Timeline of Uranus Discoveries

1787
The first of Uranus's moons are discovered.

In 1986, *Voyager 2* flew within 50,600 miles (81,433 km) of Uranus's atmosphere. The spacecraft took thousands of images. It also collected data about the planet's atmosphere, moons, and rings. The information helped scientists calculate the speed of the planet's rotation. Scientists were also able to study Uranus's magnetic field and its temperature. By 2013, both *Voyager* spacecraft were headed out of our solar system.

1986
Voyager 2 becomes the only spacecraft to fly near Uranus.

1977
Scientists first discover rings around Uranus.

2005
The most recently discovered moons of Uranus are found.

The Origin of Uranus

Powerful telescopes continue to look at Uranus. But there are other ways to study the planet today. Beyond Neptune, a cloud of small, frozen objects orbits the sun. Astronomers call this the Kuiper belt. The icy chunks may be left over from the formation of our solar system. Studying these objects can offer clues about the origin of the planets, including Uranus. What might the scientists find? With an unusual planet like Uranus, it is anyone's guess!

Some of the comets that pass by Earth may come from the Kuiper belt.

42

The Golden Record

Scientists do not know if life exists outside of Earth. But just in case it does, they placed a gold-plated disc inside both *Voyager* spacecraft. The disc includes 90 minutes of music, 115 photographs, and sounds from nature. It also includes a greeting translated into 55 different languages. If an alien civilization finds the disc, it won't have to worry about how to play it. The disc is etched with instructions.

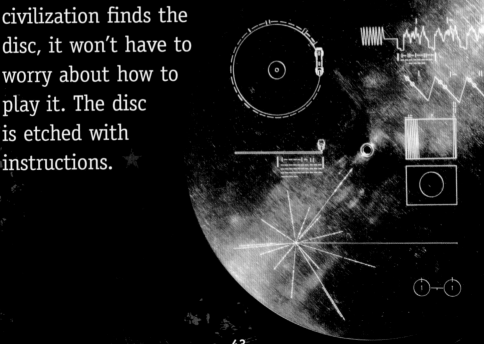

True Statistics

Number of Uranus's moons named for characters created by William Shakespeare: 24

Number of Uranus's moons named for characters created by 18th-century author Alexander Pope: 3

Largest ring around Uranus: Mu, at 60,700 mi. (97,700 km) from the center of Uranus

Smallest ring around Uranus: Zeta, at 24,600 mi. (39,600 km) from the center of Uranus

Brightest ring around Uranus: Epsilon, at 31,800 mi. (51,150 km) from the center of Uranus

Largest moon orbiting Uranus: Titania, with a 490.1 mi. (788.7 km) radius

Smallest known moon orbiting Uranus: Margaret, with a 3.7 mi. (6 km) radius

Brightest moon orbiting Uranus: Ariel, with a 359.7 mi. (578.9 km) radius

Did you find the truth?

F Uranus's core is frozen.

T *Voyager 2* is the only spacecraft to ever visit Uranus.

Resources

Books

Aguilar, David A. *13 Planets: The Latest View of the Solar System*. Washington, DC: National Geographic, 2011.

Arlon, Penelope. *Planets*. New York: Scholastic Reference, 2012.

Sparrow, Giles. *Night Sky*. New York: Scholastic Reference, 2012.

Visit this Scholastic Web site for more information on Uranus:
★ www.factsfornow.scholastic.com
Enter the keyword **Uranus**

Important Words

astronomers (uh-STRAH-nuh-mehrz) — scientists who study stars, planets, and space

atmosphere (AT-muhs-feer) — the mixture of gases that surrounds a planet

axis (AK-sis) — an imaginary line through the middle of an object, around which that object spins

comet (KAH-mit) — a bright body in outer space with a long tail

core (KOR) — the most inner part of a planet

dense (DENS) — having a large amount of matter packed tightly together

elliptical (i-LIP-tih-kuhl) — in a flat oval shape

equator (i-KWAY-tur) — an imaginary line around the middle of a planet or other body that is an equal distance from the north and south poles

hemisphere (HEM-i-sfeer) — one half of a round object, especially a planet

mass (MAS) — the amount of physical matter that an object contains

meteoroid (MEE-tee-uh-royd) — a piece of rock in space

orbits (OR-bits) — travels in a path around something, especially a planet or the sun

planet (PLAN-it) — a large body orbiting a star

Index

Page numbers in **bold** indicate illustrations

About the Author

Christine Taylor-Butler is the author of more than 65 books for children including the True Book series on American History/ Government, Health and the Human Body, and Science Experiments. A graduate of the Massachusetts Institute of Technology, Taylor-Butler holds degrees in both civil engineering and art and design. She lives in Kansas City, Missouri.

Photos ©: age fotostock/spacephotos.com: 31; Alamy Images: 38 (Richard Wainscoat), 6, 44 (Science Photo Library), 12 (Universal Images Group Limited); AP Images/North Wind Picture Archives: 34; Dreamstime/ Dannyphoto80: 14; Everett Collection/Mondadori Portfolio: 36; Getty Images/Cornell Capa/Time Life Pictures: 28; Media Bakery: back cover, 5 top, 10; NASA: 13 (Erich Karkoschka/University of Arizona), 30, 41 left (ESA/M. Showalter/SETI Institute), 24 (ESO), 27 (JPL), 18 (JPL/STScI), 22 right, 23 left (JPL/USGS), 33 (Keck Observatory), 43; National Geographic Stock: 11 (Mark Seidler), 22 all left (Steve Beshara); Science Source: 21 (Enrico Sacchetti), 4, 23 right (Jack Fields), cover, 5 bottom, 41 center (Julian Baum), 42 (Lynette Cook), 37, 40 (Maria Platt-Evans), 16, 32 (Mark Garlick), 26 (NASA), 19; Shutterstock, Inc./pixelparticle: 22 - 23 background; Superstock, Inc.: 41 right (Universal Images Group), 17 (William Radcliffe/Science Faction); The Image Works/SSPL/Jamie Cooper: 8; Wikimedia: 9 (NASA), 20, 29 (Rusliko).